THE LITTLE BOOK OF
FAERIES

MEL BARREN

summersdale

THE LITTLE BOOK OF FAERIES

An Hachette UK Company
www.hachette.co.uk

Summersdale Publishers
Part of Octopus Publishing Group Limited
Carmelite House
50 Victoria Embankment
LONDON
EC4Y 0DZ
UK

www.summersdale.com

Printed and bound in Poland

ISBN: 978-1-83799-377-2

This FSC® label means that materials used for the product have been responsibly sourced

MIX
Papper | Bidrar till
ansvarsfullt skogsbruk
FSC® C018236

✦ CONTENTS ✦

✴ INTRODUCTION ✴

Who has not been enchanted by tales of tiny faerie folk inhabiting gardens, woodlands and grassy knolls? If you've ever felt an ethereal sense of other-worldliness that you can't quite grasp, could it be that faerie folk are real and closer than you think?

We know that tales of faerie-like beings were prevalent in the ancient civilizations of Greece and Persia. People believed in the existence of human-like creatures who inhabited a parallel realm on Earth and connected with both mortals and gods. When modern religions advanced across the world, the gods and deities of the ancients were replaced by different beliefs. While the worship of fantastical gods faded into myth, tales of slightly more benign faerie folk have persisted in folklore across the world. Perhaps faeries posed no real threat to religious order, leaving storytellers, poets and local lore to speak of them.

Even today, faerie folk continue to intrigue us, perhaps because they ever-so-slightly resemble humans, but with magical powers. That may lead to the assumption that they are miniature versions of us, but woe betide any mortal who judges the faerie realm by our societal standards. Faerie – or fae – society is complex and governed by codes entirely different to our own. While many faeries are helpful and kind, they can also be capricious, temperamental and frustratingly mischievous. Entering their world, intentionally or not, can be utterly perilous.

From pixies and goblins, elves and leprechauns, to the Tooth Fairy and fairy godmothers, you will have heard of countless types of fae folk. Each type possesses a different temperament and supernatural ability. Turn the pages and explore this fascinating, nebulous world of mischief and magic. But be warned, the faerie realm is not for the faint of heart.

> "Faeries, come take me out of this dull world,
> For I would ride with you upon the wind,
> Run on the top of the dishevelled tide,
> And dance upon the mountains like a flame!"
>
> **William Butler Yeats**

CHAPTER ONE:
THE HISTORY
OF FAERIES

You are about to discover that the history of faeries is as turbulent and peculiar as the faeries themselves. Humans have used stories to explain the unknown, educate or entertain, and stories about faeries are no different. What is remarkable is that faerie lore has survived the darkest times in human history, and then flourished in creative movements.

It all began in ancient times. While aloof gods exerted power from places beyond human reach, our ancestors felt that there was another domain, here on planet Earth, where strange, magical faeries inhabited the same mountains, forests, deserts and seas as we humans. Occasionally, human and faerie paths were said to have crossed. Tales were told, and myths and superstitions were born. The finest tales became faerie lore, handed down through generations or spread from village to village, country to country. It is fortunate for us that faerie lore enthusiasts catalogued the old word-of-mouth stories. You will discover in the following pages how these tales survived and evolved, along with valuable insights into how ordinary people lived, loved and believed.

✳ WHAT IS A FAERIE? ✳

The word "faerie" immediately conjures images of tiny, winged creatures, perhaps using a magic wand to make wishes come true. This is a thoroughly modern idea. In fact, there was no reference to faeries having wings until Victorian times. In the 1920s, the artist Cicely Mary Barker enchanted the public with her paintings of "Flower Fairies", where each delicate faerie matched an exquisitely painted flower. Her faeries have little basis in lore but have captured children's hearts and imaginations for a hundred years.

Ancient faeries were rarely so cute, and were also incredibly diverse in appearance, temperament and magical ability. From sturdy Nordic dwarfs to beguiling deep-sea mermaids, these creatures seem to have little in common, except for one thing: they are all said to exist on the same planet as we mortals, but in another realm or "plane", tantalizingly just out of our reach. It is their differences that make them so utterly intriguing.

Since pagan or pre-modern religious times, faerie folklore and myths have persisted throughout Europe, the British Isles, the Nordic countries and Persia. The word "faerie" has morphed over the centuries, beginning with the Latin word *fatum* for fate, eventually evolving into Anglo-French "faerie" and Middle English "fairy".

The first written stories of faeries emerged in the twelfth century when the cleric Gervase of Tilbury shared tales of tiny, enchanted creatures with benevolent and malevolent intentions. Since then, countless storytellers, from William Shakespeare to Walt Disney, have used faerie folk as inspiration, lodging faeries even more firmly into our culture.

FAERIES AROUND THE WORLD

Across the globe, there are tales about faerie-like entities that go back millennia.

- Travel east to Japan for tales of amphibious *kappa* sprites. Unpredictable and clever, their behaviour ranges from peeking up women's kimonos and loudly breaking wind in public to drowning humans and devouring their flesh.

- The faeries of the indigenous North Americans share much in common with those on other continents and are often depicted as tiny humans. The Cherokee *yunwi tsunsdi* are helpful, while the Yana tribes tell of the man-eating *yo-yautsgi* faeries!

- In Latin America and Iberia, *duendes* are highly unpleasant characters living in caves or house walls. Depending on local lore, they have a reputation for scaring or even kidnapping children!

- In Africa, Zulu myths tell of malevolent *tokoloshe* – wicked dwarf-like faeries or spirits who make themselves invisible by placing a magic pebble in their mouths. They can be called upon to do harm to people or even cause them to die in their sleep.

- Perhaps the most beautiful creatures are the delicate *peri* of Persia, some of the few winged creatures of early faerie lore. Their ancient story is that they existed in a hinterland between gods and mortals, neither wholly evil, nor wholly saintly.

- From indigenous Australian folklore come the *Mimi* – thin, elongated faerie-like spirits who live in rocky crevices. Benevolent and wise teachers, they taught Aboriginal people how to hunt, cook, paint and make fire.

Stick a pin into any ancient map, and you will find a rich heritage of magical faerie lore. Far and wide, wherever faerie tales are told, these supernatural beings with special powers have much in common: they can bestow good or bad fortune on mortals. One thing is certain: faeries are rarely entirely benign.

✳ BEFORE THERE WERE BOOKS ✳

We've probably all encountered unsettling sounds in the forest, or spied a curious movement from the corner of our eye that has no logical explanation. The experiences of ancient peoples were no different. For centuries, the influence of supernatural faerie folk provided explanations for everyday mysteries, from a randomly bountiful apple harvest to a painful boil on the posterior. But who, or what, was responsible?

It is easy to understand how faerie lore became culturally entrenched. Why wouldn't our wild, unpredictable landscapes be inhabited by semi-human creatures who exert supernatural power over us? Tales and explanations ranged from the mundane to the extraordinary. In the true oral traditions of faerie lore, creative storytellers stimulated people's imaginations and fuelled superstitions. As illiteracy was widespread, faerie lore was passed on by word of mouth, and local tales were handed down through the generations. Other people brought stories with them as they crossed oceans, travelled lands, integrated and even marauded.

Folk and faerie lore scholars and enthusiasts have documented tales for centuries. In the tradition of oral storytelling, the teller would reserve the right to put their own spin on a tale. Because of this, variants of the same stories exist all over the world.

THE EVOLUTION OF FAERIE STORIES

Any mention of faeries at the bottom of a garden conjures images of miniature, winged humans, whereas a "crock of gold" will immediately bring to mind canny Irish leprechauns. Christmas wouldn't be Christmas without Santa's cheeky, pointy-eared elves, and who hasn't wished for a fairy godmother to grant their wishes with a wave of her wand?

Thanks to storytellers over hundreds of years, all sorts of faeries dwell in our heritage and hearts. In the following pages, we'll discover how beliefs in faeries have changed in line with human cultural evolution, but not quite as much as you might think!

TUATHA DÉ DANANN

Before there were faeries, there existed another race. Cast your imagination back to late prehistoric Ireland to a period spanning the Gaels, Druids, Celts and Romans and right up to the arrival of Christianity. Picture the Emerald Isle as home to a fantastical race of other-worldly gods skilled in magic and sorcery and immune to ageing and sickness. Legend suggests that the gods arrived on the west coast of Ireland in a vast cloud of unearthly mist. Once ashore, they burned their boats, removing their own escape route and forcing them to settle in a permanent homeland. The *Tuatha Dé Danann* had arrived.

Tuatha Dé Danann translates as "The people of the Goddess Danu". Danu is the pagan mother of the gods; she and her tribe of gods shared their skills and lived among the mortals.

For a while, there was peace and good health for all, but, inevitably, power struggles and battles between the Otherworld and mortals ensued. Eventually the *Tuatha Dé Danann* were defeated by the ancestors of Ireland's Celtic people, the Milesians.

The *Tuatha Dé Danann* were driven through portals in ancient burial sites to live underground.

According to legend, there they remain, abiding by their own codes and invisible to mortals. In the post-Christian context, Ireland's medieval monks diligently recorded the folklore tales but with a religious slant. The *Tuatha Dé Danann* were described as fallen angels rather than gods. The monks acknowledged their other-worldly powers but said that their lack of Christian faith diminished their physical stature. This is the point at which towering gods became wee faerie folk.

FALLEN FAERIE ANGELS

As Christianity spread across Europe and Scandinavia, faerie lore adopted a religious slant more fitting to the times. Many old tales persisted, but faeries came to be thought of as angels who had fallen from grace, or deceased heathens not quite wicked enough to enter Hell or saintly enough to enter Heaven. A good example are the pixies of south-west England, who came to be defined as faeries created from the souls of unbaptized dead infants.

THE CANTERBURY TALES

In the fourteenth century, the English poet Geoffrey Chaucer wrote *The Canterbury Tales*, a collection of tales told by fictional pilgrims travelling to Canterbury Cathedral. Even then, in medieval Britain, one of the pilgrims spoke wistfully about times past, when faeries roamed the land:

> "When good King Arthur ruled in ancient days,
> (A king that every Briton loves to praise.)
> This was a land brim-full of fairy folk."
>
> **Geoffrey Chaucer, "The Wife of Bath"**

DANGEROUS TIMES

From around 1400 to the mid-1700s, any belief with supernatural or other-worldly connotations was dangerous. In an act of social self-preservation in a climate of fervent religious oppression, the faeries of old that people had believed in for hundreds of years were trivialized into mere stories...

That said, beliefs were not entirely eradicated, for families still told faerie stories around the fire, children sang nursery rhymes about faeries, and scholars far and wide documented faerie lore.

KING JAMES VI

In 1597, the Jacobean King James VI of Scotland (later also James I of England and Ireland) published three books entitled *Dæmonologie*. The books describe in detail demons (dæmons), witches and sorcerers. He was deeply concerned that the "black arts" opposed Christian values – and his own position – which meant that anyone suspected of dealing with demons, witchcraft and even faeries was in mortal danger.

These were paranoid times. Witch-hunting had proliferated for some 200 years, and with this publication, things got even worse for anyone who may have believed in faeries.

King James's books added fuel to the witchcraft fire (quite literally), and women were especially endangered. In *The Thirde Booke of Dæmonologie*, he turned his attention to spirits, faeries and brownies, declaring that they were demons in disguise who possessed ungodly people ignorant enough to engage with them. He stated:

> "The deuil illuded the senses of sundry simple creatures, in making them beleeue that they saw and harde such thinges as were nothing so indeed."

It was mostly women who were vulnerable to cruel, often fatal punishments. King James believed that females were inherently less rational than males and, therefore, more likely to fall for faerie or demonic trickery and manipulation. If a woman was accused of dealing with faeries or demons, local magistrates had the power to hand out atrocious "cures" or even death sentences.

Now enshrined in King James's books, a sinister shift to long-held beliefs about faeries took hold. The King decreed that common misfortune – from a sudden illness to a failed crop – was the fault of the individual, who had undoubtedly been ignorant and ungodly enough to let faerie or demonic spirits enter them. Even infant birth defects did not escape suspicion, for surely they were a sign that the mother had cavorted with faeries, spirits or demons.

During these dark times no one was truly safe. As faeries became associated with the very dangerous business of witchcraft and the Devil, it was perilous to engage with anything deemed supernatural or to accept deities other than the Christian god.

But beliefs and superstitions about faeries were so entrenched in the psyches of ordinary people that talk of them did not disappear. Instead, faeries came to be regarded as mere fictional characters rather than beings with mystical powers. Things were safer that way!

ROBERT KIRK

Reverend Robert Kirk (9 December 1644–14 May 1692) was a Scottish minister, Gaelic scholar and folklorist. His collection of folklore was collated into the book *The Secret Commonwealth of Elves, Fauns and Fairies*, in which he documented Scottish folklore and traditional beliefs about supernatural beings.

The book systematically recorded faerie lore, witchcraft, ghosts and the gift of "second sight" (which is the ability to predict or foretell the future through visions or dreams). At the time, ordinary people from the Scottish Highlands who dabbled in the folklore of their culture were being harshly accused of practising dark magic and witchcraft by the Presbyterian courts.

The title page for his original book, written in his own hand, says: "The Secret Common-Wealth OR A treatise displaying the chief curiosities among the people of Scotland as they are in use to this day."

Kirk died just before the book was published. One evening, he took his usual pre-bedtime walk on Doon Hill (a place rumoured to be where faeries dwell) in his nightgown. His dead body was found lying on the hill. Very quickly, lore emerged, purporting that his corpse was not actually buried in his tomb because the faeries had taken him away.

To this day, a tree on Doon Hill is rumoured to be the entrance to Faerieland. People attach notes, wishes and requests to the tree, asking the faeries for help with their hopes and dreams or to care for their deceased loved ones.

THE ROMANTIC MOVEMENT

In the early 1800s, a movement that became known as Romanticism developed across Europe. This creative and intellectual celebration of the natural world through music, painting and literature was posited as the "cure" to Victorian mass industrialization and social upheaval. It glorified a gentler past, drawing on flora and fauna and medieval legends. Faeries, an enchantment of the natural world, were a rich source of subject matter.

THE GENESIS OF MODERN FAERIE TALES

In Germany, the Brothers Grimm, dedicated cataloguers of faerie tales, remastered a collection of traditional stories, initially for an adult audience. The first edition was published in 1812 with astonishing success. Some tales were of such cruelty that the brothers republished toned-down versions over the next three decades.

Meanwhile, in Denmark in 1836, Hans Christian Andersen rewrote *The Little Mermaid* as part of a volume of faerie stories specifically for children, adapting traditional versions of the tale. Although there was less grisly violence, the faerie mermaid's outcome remained bittersweet. In 1989, Walt Disney gave the story a radical makeover, complete with a happily-ever-after ending.

VICTORIAN FAERIES

Arguably, our modern interpretation of faeries is influenced by Victorian ideas. The public sustained a keen appetite for folklore, mythology and the supernatural throughout Queen Victoria's reign (1837–1901) and into King Edward VII's reign until 1910.

Various creative movements took hold. The Arts and Crafts Movement stimulated a historical interest in ancient lore and craft. Faeries were popularized, and were often idealized as the ethereal, floaty beings we know today.

THE CELTIC REVIVAL

The Celtic Revival, another cultural and artistic movement, unfolded in the late nineteenth century. Primarily taking root in Ireland and Scotland, the movement aimed to restore, preserve and celebrate Celtic customs, folklore, artistry and ancestral language.

The movement was a direct response to the erosion of traditional culture under modern influences. The Celtic Revival helped to stimulate a public fascination with Celtic myth, faerie lore and folklore alongside a resurgence of interest in the historic arts and crafts of Ireland, Scotland and Wales.

PRE-RAPHAELITE CONTROVERSY

In Victorian England, the Pre-Raphaelites were a group of artists and poets who expressed their yearning for more romantic days. Much of their work was inspired by Greek and medieval legends. They paid meticulous attention to the natural world in all its glory, and their controversial paintings and words dripped with symbolism and romance. They were acclaimed by some critics and lambasted as morally shocking by others.

In the sixteenth century, under the influence of the artist Raphael, grandeur and structure became the accepted standard for art. Approved topics included religion, science, architecture and human achievement. Myth, legend, and, indeed, faeries were considered unsuitable subjects.

Given the freedom of artistic expression today, it is hard to comprehend how disruptive the Pre-Raphaelites were in the nineteenth century. Holman Hunt painted faeries and Christina Rossetti wrote the famous poem *Goblin Market*, with both receiving a mixture of societal applause and critical outrage. The Pre-Raphaelite movement eventually disbanded, but only after it had inspired others to draw on the natural world and use old lore as a rich source of material.

W. B. YEATS, POET AND FOLKLORIST

Eminent personalities linked to the Celtic Revival include the Irish writer and poet W. B. Yeats. His collection of folklore, *Fairy and Folk Tales of the Irish Peasantry*, published in 1888, helped to popularize traditional Irish faerie tales and contributed to a widespread fascination with all things supernatural from Celtic culture.

Yeats fired imaginations with fascinating, vivid stories about faeries, leprechauns, ghosts and other mystical characters. His writing gave a much broader audience rich insight into Irish folklore and superstitions.

IOLANTHE

Gilbert and Sullivan's satirical comic opera *Iolanthe* premiered in London in 1882. The opera pokes fun at Queen Victoria and British society through the tale of forbidden love between mortals and faeries.

The play was a huge success and had an interesting by-product. The inventor of the incandescent light bulb, Joseph Swan, was tasked with creating miniature lights to attach to the lead faerie's costume. When a rival inventor strung the lights around a Christmas tree, "faerie lights" were established as the festive tradition that we know and love today.

FROM THE NINETEENTH CENTURY TO PRESENT DAY

J. M. Barrie's play *Peter Pan* was staged in 1904. Peter Pan's faerie sidekick was a possessive little creature called Tinker Bell. Her personality gave more than a nod to a typical faerie's capricious nature. Mr Barrie was clearly well read in faerie lore, as was the astoundingly talented Arthur Rackham, who illustrated the *Peter Pan* book.

After Barrie's work, faeries gained more and more attention. Throughout the twentieth century, Walt Disney popularized many faerie stories through the success of his animated films. In 1937, J. R. R. Tolkien redefined the fantasy genre with his faerie-tale-inspired novel, *The Hobbit*. During the rest of the twentieth century, many faerie-like creatures entered mainstream culture, including movies, books and video games. In the 1980s, there was an explosion of faerie-fantasy films, such as *The Dark Crystal* (1982), *The NeverEnding Story* (1984), and *Labyrinth* (1986). And in 1997, again paying close attention to myth and lore, J. K. Rowling's first *Harry Potter* book brought ancient magical types (including faeries) to a whole new audience. Children and adults were gripped!

OUR NEVER-ENDING FAERIE TALE

As we have learned, for our ancient ancestors, gods, mythical creatures and even faeries were accepted as existing. Across oceans and continents, most early civilizations seem to have believed in something "other".

We owe much to the people who passed on faerie stories through word of mouth and to the insightful enthusiasts who catalogued faerie lore and tales of old. They kept these stories alive, and our fascination with them has barely dwindled. Thanks to the power of storytelling, faeries – from benevolent fairy godmothers to wicked faerie queens – are so familiar to us that a scene-setting backstory is rarely required. Good or bad, we already know them very well. Tales about enchanted beings have endured for millennia, and our relationship and fascination with faeries shows no sign of diminishing.

CHAPTER TWO:
THE LEGENDS
OF FAE

Fortunately, many tales have been retold repeatedly or have been adapted into movies and so are familiar to us. We all know something of the Legend of King Arthur (where faeries play a pivotal role), but have you heard of the terrifying faerie hounds with a taste for mortals? How about the merman with a taste for whiskey?

The legends are not just about the faeries themselves. Just as the mythical faerie kingdom of Avalon is central to King Arthur's legend, the location of faerie realms is just as shrouded in tantalizing lore. As capricious, unpredictable and varied as the faeries themselves, faerie legends are not reserved for noble deeds and good versus evil tropes, nor do they illustrate a moralistic point. Far from it! Often, the legends brim with darkness, wit or mischief. One thing is sure: these legends are curious, bizarre... and never dull, as you are about to see.

✦ **WHAT IS A LEGEND?** ✦

Legends usually – but not always – have some basis in historical fact. The tales often have a moral but are typically peppered with unprovable or improbable aspects. This turns a simple story of good versus evil into legends that endure for centuries.

Robin Hood is a fine example of a legend. The story of a witty thief and his band of Merry Men who steal from the rich and give to the poor is a legend that has been retold for 600 years. It is believed that the character of Robin Hood was based on a number of real historical figures dating back to the late thirteenth century. The High Sheriff of Nottinghamshire certainly existed, and both men obtained legendary status.

FAERIE LORE

Lore – in this case, faerie lore – are tales accumulated over time and passed down from generation to generation. Local customs, superstitions and beliefs are often woven into the lore.

BLURRED LINES

While many tales involving faeries have little (if any) factual foundation, some do relate to historical events or real people. Those fall into the category of faerie legend. Stories with no proven historical lineage are usually characterized as faerie lore. That said, the line between legend and lore is not definitive, particularly as the very nature of oral storytelling means that tales might well have been exaggerated! Take what you will from faerie legend and lore. The stories may simply entertain you, or you may feel that there's some truth in these thousands of enchanting and enduring narratives.

FACT, FICTION AND BELIEVERS

Plenty of modern people believe in faeries, and a handful claim to have seen them. They care not whether stories about these supernatural beings are legend or lore. Proceed with an open mind and in these pages you will discover vivid and fascinating tales from an entirely different frontier.

✷ THE LEGEND OF KING ARTHUR ✷

Camelot. The very word conjures visions of magnificent castle turrets rising from the mist, of dragons, faeries, wizards, and of magic from an other-worldly time.

Legend tells of a boy named Arthur in fifth-century Britain. He pulled the magic sword Excalibur from a stone and became king. However, evidence of his existence is inconclusive! Even if he did exist, whether he was a king is also debatable. There is not even any evidence that his castle, Camelot, was real. In another twist, he is said to have died on the mythical faerie island of Avalon. Arthurian enthusiasts suggest that Avalon is located in Glastonbury, in south-west England.

THE LADY OF THE LAKE

The Lady of the Lake plays a pivotal role in King Arthur's legend. Depending on the version of the tale, she is named Viviane or Nimue and rose from the watery depths holding Excalibur, Arthur's magical sword, and was involved in the demise of the powerful wizard Merlin. Depending on the retelling – and there are many – Merlin loved Viviane/Nimue and schooled her in the art of powerful magic. Some versions are that she killed Merlin to free herself from his clutches, or that she killed Merlin so that she could replace him as Arthur's advisor. The Lady of the Lake is sometimes described as a benevolent faerie nymph from an underwater realm or a faerie-like enchantress in human form.

King Arthur is said to lie in Avalon. The Lady of the Lake helped transport the dying king across the lake where he still lies guarded by four faerie queens. Legend foretells that Arthur will rise again when humanity needs him most.

> "Willows whiten, aspens quiver,
> Little breezes dusk and shiver
> Through the wave that runs for ever
> By the island in the river"
> **Alfred, Lord Tennyson**

✳ PEOPLE OF THE MOUNDS ✳

Daoine sìdhe, pronounced "dee-nuh shee", is Scottish Gaelic for "people of the mounds" (it's also given as *aos sí*, pronounced "ays sheeth-uh", in Irish Gaelic). In Scottish folklore, these are supernatural faerie beings who live deep inside hills and mounds. It is said that they descended from the pagan gods *Tuatha Dé Danann*, who were driven underground by our human ancestors (see page 14).

Not just confined to underground provinces, they are said to also be active above ground, especially at sunset or after midnight. Seasonally, there can be "flittings" – or processions – when entire communities move from one mound to another. If two *daoine sìdhe* tribes cross paths, there are ferocious battles. In Scotland, when yellow lichen turns red after the first frosts, it is fabled to be the spilled blood of warring factions.

QUARTER DAY FESTIVITIES

To honour the natural cycles of the Earth, they are especially active outside on Quarter Days. These consist of the winter and summer solstices and spring and autumn equinoxes. They play music, dance, drink and feast with great enthusiasm in the open air.

ONE EVENING LASTS MANY YEARS

It is an unfortunate mortal who is enticed to join *daoine sìdhe* festivities. Time moves differently in the Otherworld. A single evening spent with the *daoine sìdhe* may be much longer in human terms. People who accept *daoine sìdhe* hospitality return home the next day to find that their family have aged by decades or have died long ago. There might be strangers living in their house, or they might return to discover that no one alive even remembers them.

Those who escape the frolics and return to their everyday lives can never find happiness again. Everything seems dull, joyless and lacklustre. These people either fade away, pining for the Otherworld or waste their days obsessively searching for the way back to the faerie realm.

THE MERRY MERROW AND THE LOST SOULS

A merrow is a type of scaly, green faerie merman who wears a magic red cap that gives them the power to breathe in the sea or air. One legend tells of a man from the west coast of Ireland. His name was Jack Dougherty and he had been told tales by his late grandfather of a friendly merrow called Coomera and how they used to drink and sing songs together.

After gazing out to sea on many an occasion, one misty day Jack finally saw Coomara boldly standing on a rock. They immediately became friends. Coomara put a magic red cap on Jack's head, and together they dived to the bottom of the sea to Coomara's surprisingly warm and cosy home.

They drank heartily from barrels of "sunken whiskey" that had been lost in shipwrecks. They laughed, sang songs, and reminisced fondly about Jack's grandfather. Jack noticed rows of lobster pots in Coomara's home. It turned out that the cold and frightened souls of drowned sailors would seek refuge in Coomara's cosy home, and it amused him to lock the souls in lobster pots.

Jack was horrified and formulated a plan. He invited Coomara to visit his home the following week and try home-made *potcheen*, a potent potato whiskey. The *potcheen* made Coomara so drunk that he passed out under Jack's table.

Jack stole Coomara's red cap, ran to the shore and dived into the briny waves. He swam to Coomara's home and gently freed the trapped souls, careful not to disturb the lobster pots. When he returned home Coomara was still under the table and none the wiser. The two of them remained drinking buddies for many years. Still, occasionally, Jack would get Coomara drunk enough so he could borrow the magic cap and sneak off to free more souls.

THE LEGEND OF KNOCKSHEGOWNA

This legend tells of a battle of wits between a canny young man and an outraged faerie queen. It all began with a farmer in Knockshegowna, Ireland, who gazed mournfully upon a lush, green faerie hill as his diminishing cattle herd, stricken by sickness, grazed on the scrubby lowland. At night, he could hear music as the faeries danced on their fertile hill.

Several hired herdsmen tried to graze cows on the faerie hill, but when the cows trampled and chewed the green grass, the faerie queen was having none of it. She played out a cunning plan many times over with great success.

After dark, she would appear before the herdsman. Their eyes glued open by magical powers, they could not look away as the faerie queen danced, whirled, and then shapeshifted into hideous monstrous beings – a giant owl with eyes of fire, a spitting serpent with the body of a wolf, a snorting black bull with seven heads, each manifestation louder and more abominable than before. Meanwhile, the cattle were driven mad, stampeding into ditches or bewitched and unable to stop running.

A canny young man with a three-cornered hat and a set of musical pipes offered to help the farmer in return for bed, board and beer for the rest of his days. The desperate farmer shook his hand and sealed the deal.

The young man led the cows to pasture on the faerie hill and settled down to play his pipes. As the moon rose, the faerie queen appeared, at first beautiful and then more hideous with each shapeshifting manifestation. Bemused, he invited her to do her worst. When her worst failed, she tried another tactic, becoming a docile creamy calf with gentle brown eyes. As she sidled up to him, he leapt on her back, knowing that a faerie must do your bidding if you take hold of them.

Accepting that she had been outwitted, she honourably vowed to leave the hill, and no faeries would ever return. Of course, the young man led an easy life with the farmer's hospitality, and they all lived happily ever after.

SCOTLAND'S
MONSTROUS FAERIE HOUND

Not all faeries resemble humans, nor are all faeries small in size. In Scotland, *cù-sìth* translates to "Faerie Dog" and is an ominous, terrifying hound and harbinger of death. *Cù-sìth* guards the gateways to faerie kingdoms and is as large as a highland cow, with green shaggy fur, glowing red eyes and a coiled tail.

A vulnerable mortal out in the open and unlucky enough to hear a blood-curdling *cù-sìth* howl must find safe shelter – and fast! Howls come in threes. The third – and most chilling – howl can cause death from sheer terror. *Cù-sìth* then collects the soul and delivers it to the faerie Otherworld.

Nursing mothers were prized by *cù-sìth* and, as a consequence, were locked indoors after sunset. Drawn by the smell of milk and nursing babies, *cù-sìth* prowls after dark in search of new mothers to abduct. Captured mothers are taken to a faerie mound to provide rich milk for *daoine sìdhe* faerie children.

THE LEGEND OF
THOMAS THE RHYMER

Thomas de Ercildoun was a real thirteenth-century laird, born in Berwickshire in 1220. Legend has it that he was romantically entwined with a faerie queen.

It is said that the Queen of Elfland became enamoured with Sir Thomas after meeting him in a forest. She carried him off to Faerieland on a white faerie horse with nine and 50 bells on its mane.

> "They have sought him high and sought him low,
> They have sought him over down and lea,
> They have found him by the milk-white thorn
> That guards the gates o' Faerie."
>
> **Rudyard Kipling,**
> **"The Last Rhyme of True Thomas"**

After seven joyous years together, the time came for Thomas to return to the mortal world. Before his departure, the Queen bestowed him with two very mixed faerie blessings: the gift of prophecy and the inability to tell a lie. His story and prophecies inspired ballads and poems for centuries after his death in around 1298. He is said to have even prophesied the death of the Scottish king Alexander III.

✴ **WHERE IS FAERIELAND?** ✴

According to the legends, entire faerie kingdoms are said to appear and disappear from view, like gossamer realms on a parallel plane to ours. Not bound by the same physics inflicted on the human realm, fae folk can, like us, dwell above ground, but unlike us they also live in faerie kingdoms and cities deep inside mountains and hills or underwater in rivers and oceans.

While you may never find the entrance to a faerie kingdom, lore and fable indicate you may be closer to the faerie realm than you dare believe.

Read on to discover more about these faerie kingdoms.

DISAPPEARING ISLANDS

Often, faerie kingdoms are islands or provinces just out of reach to mortals. Off the west coast of Ireland, in the wild Atlantic Ocean and shrouded by mist and fog, lies the mythical island of Hy-Brasil, which materializes every seven years... and then fades away. It was shown on maps right up until 1873.

To this very day, the Isle of Man in the Irish Sea is steeped in faerie lore. Cloaked in a blue fog, the entire island was said to be invisible to sailors until the first humans were shipwrecked on its shores.

THE WELSH OTHERWORLD

In Wales, *Annwn* (also known as *Annwfn* or *Annwfyn*) translates to "very deep place" and is considered to be part of the Otherworld. Complete with castles, kings and queens, it was believed to lie north of the shrouded Welsh mountains and later thought to be beyond the craggy Pembrokeshire coast. Just like the end of the rainbow, no mortal could determine its exact location.

SCOTLAND'S FAERIE MOUNDS

Across Scotland, there is a rich heritage of faerie folk who live freely in the forests. Other fae access vast, deep kingdoms through concealed entrances in any one of the numerous faerie mounds – or grassy hills and hillocks – scattered across Scotland's wild terrain.

SCANDI OTHERWORLDS

Travel to Iceland and the Faroe Islands, even today, and you'll hear tell that it is a reckless person who throws stones, because they might hit the *huldufólk* – or "hidden people" – whose kingdom is an underground otherworld. But they aren't just confined below ground, they are also rumoured to live within the forests, the lava fields and the rocky terrain.

AVALON

Perhaps the most enduring of all faerie kingdoms is that from the previously mentioned Legend of King Arthur, fabled to be laid to rest in Avalon, a province deep inside a faerie hill. Avalon is said to be in Glastonbury – "The Isle of Glass" – in the west of England, where the Glastonbury Tor once protruded from the watery landscape like a misty island.

SEA KINGDOMS

Across Europe and Scandinavia, tales are told of entire palaces that lie below the waves and are home to the merpeople. Other legends tell of merpeople who inhabit the mythical lost city of Atlantis.

NORDIC SUBTERRANEAN DWARFS

In Norse mythology, dwarfs live and work underground. Over time, they became associated with mining, along with other types of faeries also believed to inhabit mines.

SOLITARY FAERIES

Some faeries do not live in a specific kingdom, since faeries can live anywhere in nature, in small groups or alone in trees, flowers and rivers. Bluebells, elder and hawthorn trees hold particular reverence as faerie habitats.

FRESHWATER FAERIES

In Japan, individual demonic *kappa* sprites live in pools and rivers; lonely goat-legged urisks are found by isolated Scottish pools and riverbanks; and in Germany and Scandinavia, mischievous shapeshifting Nixies live in rivers, lakes and wells.

HOUSE FAERIES

Some faeries such as brownies even adopt a house or family and live indoors. For the lucky households, brownies help with the chores. In a few unlucky ones, malevolent boggarts move in. They are horribly disruptive, throwing pots and causing chaos! Just as unpleasant are the *duendes* of Mexico – hideous goblin-like creatures who live inside walls and come out at night to terrorize children.

It is fair to say that Faerieland is everywhere and nowhere, below and above, near and yet far away.

CHAPTER THREE:
FAERIE
CHARACTERISTICS

Things are about to become very strange, especially as the faeries of lore are not the cute winged creatures of picture books and animated cartoons. As a species, faeries are diverse and complex.

Their characteristics are aligned with their natural habitat. In wild and hostile terrains, fae folk are less likely to be pretty or friendly. In a green meadow or woodland, faeries such as pixies or leprechauns may resemble humans. Selkie sea faeries around the Orkney Islands resemble playful seals. In contrast, North European dwarfs are sturdy artisans who dwell inside rugged mountains.

Their main concern, common to the entire species, is to not interact with humans. Surprising as it might seem, most of them, apart from house faeries, care little for us. While some may help humans if they feel like it, others may wilfully hinder or harm us if we get in their way. Frankly, they have quite enough going on in their own worlds to keep them busy. Expect the unexpected as we discover more about these strange creatures.

✦ WHAT *EXACTLY* ARE FAERIES? ✦

Faeries are usually described as mythical creatures with magical powers. If only it were that simple! To elaborate, they are often said to be supernatural beings distinctly different from angels, elementals, gods, demons and ghosts. They exist in a separate realm – or plane – sometimes overlapping with other realms, including ours.

THE FAERIE HINTERLAND

Faeries inhabit a hinterland somewhere between angels and humans. Lore and legend describe thousands of types of faeries. Their homelands, characteristics and appearance vary wildly from the little winged characters we are familiar with today to the wild and untamed creatures of ancient faerie lore.

MAGIC AND MISCHIEF

As much as their physical appearance varies, so do their magical powers and personalities.

Many can shapeshift or make themselves invisible. Some can turn gold into leaves if it is in the wrong hands. Others can magically do the chores of ten farm labourers. While their powers are varied and plentiful, they rarely, if ever, have a wand!

GOOD FAERIES
AND BAD FAERIES

The "good versus evil" story trope is as old as time. Every civilization, faith and culture has tales where one overcomes the other, and fae culture is no different. Except that, of course, it's not that simple! "Good" and "bad" for faeries is more complex and nuanced than it is in human society.

In Scotland, a helpful way exists to categorize faeries by dividing them into distinct camps, or "courts". They use the Gaelic word "seelie", which means holy, benevolent or good. "unseelie" means unholy or unblessed.

THE SEELIE COURT (THE GOOD GUYS)

Members of the Seelie Court are mostly benevolent. Their interactions with mortals are generally positive. They may bring people good luck or even help them with chores. Faeries from the Seelie Court may also bestow upon people they feel are worthy the gifts of healing, musicianship or artistry.

Of course, there are caveats; fae codes of conduct and morality differ significantly from ours. Reprisals may be handed out if a fae is offended or wronged by mortal beings. Faeries are private and secretive. If they help a human, it is on condition that the human never speaks of the faerie or the nature of the help. Severe retribution will be dispensed if the contract is broken by gossip or bragging. This is fair play under Seelie Court codes. Even the most friendly Seelie Court members may occasionally be mischievous or play pranks, but that does not necessarily make them members of the Unseelie Court.

THE UNSEELIE COURT (THE BAD GUYS)

The Unseelie Court is the darker and malevolent counterpart to the kindly fae in the Seelie Court. Unseelie Court members are associated with spite, violence and wickedness.

They may engage in harmful activities towards humans for their own sport, such as stealing away babies and nursing mothers. Twilight is an especially risky time for hapless mortals to be out in the open as this is when unseelies are believed to come out to play! It is, however, worth noting that not all unseelies are downright evil, but their actions are often harmful.

✳ **FAERIE SOCIETIES** ✳

Broadly speaking, faerie societies fall into three categories, which can be divided again into light or dark (seelie or unseelie) faeries. Good or evil, the three categories are:

- Trooping faeries who live in groups.
- Solitary faeries who live and operate alone.
- Domestic faeries who live in human homes.

TROOPING FAERIES

These faeries live together in groups and communities. Their home may be underground in a kingdom or village or in the open in woodlands and mountains. Trooping faeries often travel as a group, most likely in processions or faerie circles where they dance, sing and play music.

> "By the moon we sport and play,
> With the night begins our day;
> As we dance, the dew doth fall;
> Trip it, little urchins all,

> Lightly as the little Bee,
> Two by two and three by three:
> And about go we, and about go we."

Anonymous, *The Maid's Metamorphosis* **(c. 1600)**

It is important to understand when troopings might occur in order to avoid them. Even Seelie Court fae do not like troopings to be observed by humans. It may be tempting to join in, but you will be entering their realm and may find yourself so enchanted that you wish never to return home.

Faerie trooping processions can happen anytime, but the most impressive and celebratory troopings occur on:

- The full moon.

- Both equinoxes (where day and night are equal in time).

- Both solstices (the shortest day in winter and the longest day in summer).

- Beltane (some time in May).

- Samhain (around the end of October).

Beltane is an ancient Celtic festival celebrated midway between spring and summer, known as May Day in modern calendars. Beltane marks the beginning of the light half of the year and is associated with fertility, bonfires and dancing.

Samhain is midway between autumn and winter. It marks the start of the dark half of the year, celebrated around the end of October on the dark moon or new moon. It is a time to honour the dead and the coming winter. Halloween on 31 October has its roots in the ancient Samhain festival.

Faeries may also troop seasonally when they move to their winter or summer home. If rival faerie communities happen to meet along the way, they may battle ferociously. Blood will be spilled!

SOLITARY FAERIES

The Solitaries are the fae folk who live alone or in tight family groups. It is generally thought that they should be avoided – many are said to be malicious, even murderous. They usually live in pits, ditches or marshes. Whether they are all solitary by choice is debatable. The hairy and naked Manx fenodyree was a house brownie banished from the faerie court for making love to a mortal woman.

Will-o'-the-wisps are another solitary species. They glow mysteriously over marshy ground, leading travellers astray. Germanic Nixies are lone freshwater faeries (similar to sea-dwelling merpeople) found in rivers and pools. Some Nixies are helpful to humans, while others are dangerous and will lure people to a watery grave. The shapeshifting *púca* of Ireland roam the countryside and moors, terrorizing travellers and small children.

Others are not quite so fear-inducing, with leprechauns being a good example. They mend and make shoes for trooping faeries in exchange for faerie gold but are otherwise reasonably solitary. But if you're out alone in faerie territory, the advice is to tread with caution!

DOMESTIC FAERIES

Domestic, or house faeries, are usually solitary and adopt a human household. Occasionally, if the home is large enough – perhaps a castle or a sizeable farm – a small family of brownies may work together, but that is unusual.

Most domestic faeries care little about their appearance. They are generally bedraggled, skinny, sometimes hairy, and wear only simple rags. Dobby the house elf, for those familiar with the *Harry Potter* books, is a wonderful representation of a domestic faerie, with his sackcloth tunic and bare feet.

By nature, domestic faeries are unassuming creatures, labouring for others in return for a humble meal and a floor to sleep upon. But be warned! If a domestic faerie is offended or insulted, they are prone to unleashing acts of horrible malice.

Some types of domestic or house faeries are:

- Brownies
- Boggarts
- Dobies
- *Duendes*

UNDERSTANDING OUR DIFFERENCES

Our rules simply don't apply to faeries, and why should they? Faeries are said to exist in a domain on Earth that is nigh impossible for us to comprehend, so it is little wonder that their society and values do not mirror ours. Our differences are profound.

IN DEFIANCE OF PHYSICS

Faeries defy the Newtonian laws of physics. They can move through seemingly solid obstacles. They can shapeshift into different physical forms. Even time and space behave differently in their realm. Many fae move three-dimensionally, flying through the air or living underwater. How, then, could we possibly think of them simply as winged, tiny versions of us?

FAERIES AND NATURE

While industrialization diminished human connection to the environment, faeries remain intertwined with their natural habitat and are reportedly fiercely protective of it. Their home, community and food source exist in their immediate surroundings.

Many flowers and trees are associated with potent faerie magic. A cradle carved from the elder tree will alert the faeries to visit and pinch the infant until it is black and blue. In the days before we imagined faeries with wings, it was thought that they flew through the air riding on the stems of a ragwort plant.

UNTAMED AND WILD

To modern-day humans, faerie behaviour is as raw, unpredictable and untamed as the wind. Their quick tempers and zest for enjoyment are almost toddler-like to us, but to think that would be to underestimate them.

While we may not always understand faerie behaviour, legend suggests that to insult them or spoil their surroundings is to risk vengeful and cunning mischief or retribution, and there is nothing childlike about that. Humans have blamed tangled hair, nightmares, rheumatism, stroke – and even death – on affronted faeries.

✳ **PROTECTION FROM FAERIES** ✳

It seems that humans have not always fully grasped the complex codes governing faerie behaviour. Not all faeries are believed to be troublesome, but there is a lot of hearsay, and superstitions are rife. The general advice has always been to maintain a respectful distance from the fae. Old faerie lore is full of ideas on repelling, deterring or discouraging faerie attention. If keeping a distance is impossible, or if venturing through known faerie territory at night is unavoidable, there are some recommended protection tactics:

PERSONAL PROTECTION

- **Iron**: Carry an iron nail or wear iron jewellery.

- **Rowan**: Pop some rowan berries or leaves in a coat pocket.

- **Clothing**: Wear clothes inside out as this confuses faeries.

- **Red cloth**: Attach a scrap of red cloth to outerwear.

- **Red thread**: Tie red thread around babies' chests.

HOME PROTECTION

- **Red ribbon**: Tie a red ribbon on the front door.

- **Flax**: Hang a dried bunch from the ceiling, or place fresh flax flowers in a vase.

- **St John's Wort**: Hang a sprig of St John's Wort in the doorway.

- **Verbena**: Hang sprigs above the threshold.

- **Salt**: Sprinkle salt on the floor and windowsills to ward off land-dwelling faeries.

- **Iron**: Hang an iron horseshoe above the threshold.

- **Shoes**: Place shoes with the toes pointing away from the bed.

- **One sock**: Place a single sock under the bed.

- **Black cockerel**: This fowl in a yard strikes terror into faeries.

- **Booming bells**: Ring large, deep-toned bells, especially church bells.

- **Stones with holes**: Hang the stones with thread above stable doors to repel faerie horse "borrowers".

- **Good manners**: For those who receive help from a house faerie, never criticize their work.

RESPECT AND AVOID

Fae folk are said to be easily offended by our blundering human ways. For example, few places feel as enchanted as a bluebell wood. Hushed, heavy in perfume, and dark, it is easy to imagine that faeries are close by. Protective of their environment, they are said to cast spells on careless humans who destroy or trample on those precious flowers. Here are some ways to avoid this:

- Treat the natural environment respectfully.

- Stay away from known faerie lands.

- Do not cross faerie ground on the solstices or equinoxes.

- Never throw stones anywhere in Iceland or the Faroe Islands.

- Never damage or step into a faerie ring of mushrooms.

- Regardless of how alluring it looks, never, ever gatecrash faerie festivities.

- Picking elderflowers from an elder tree on Midsummer's Eve will see you abducted to Faerieland for seven years.

✳ FAERIE ETIQUETTE ✳

Good manners are prized, but beware! You will not be surprised to learn that our rules do not apply and that faerie manners are a minefield. As an example of just how complex faerie etiquette is, know that a polite "thank you" may mean one thing to us, but to the fae means that you are indebted to them. It is better to say "I am grateful" instead.

THE UNGRATEFUL FARMER

Over-generosity, when humans try to express gratitude, is a common failing and can cause offence, as in the case of the poor widow (see page 81). House brownies, for example, are diligent, hard workers, expecting little for their efforts except fresh cream and bread with honey. They don't expect gifts or high praise, just kind respect. On the other hand, being critical can also lead to problems. In one old English faerie story, an insensitive farmer criticized a brownie's method of threshing wheat, only to find his entire crop hurled off a cliff. The offended (and offending) brownie angrily departed and was never seen again.

✳ OTHER RULES ✳

- Bragging is a trait faeries abhor. A recipient of faerie help must never boast or mention it to another person.

- Never break a promise to a faerie.

- Never, ever say their name or tell them yours.

✳ THE F-WORD ✳

Never, ever call them "faeries"! Centuries-old superstitions of offending the faeries or attracting their attention led to a fear of mentioning them by name.

Did you know that names carry magic powers? In fae culture, names are considered to be part of one's identity. Names are imbued with magic and belong to the owner as personal property. The fae believe that you have power over them if you speak just their given name, let alone even utter the blanket term "faerie".

Now flip that around. If a faerie knows *your* name, they can use it in spells and enchantments against you – so keep it to yourself!

FAERIE NAMES AND THE TALE OF RUMPELSTILTSKIN

In Germany in 1812, Jacob and Wilhelm Grimm, otherwise known as the Brothers Grimm, published their version of the old folk tale *Rumpelstiltskin*. This well-known faerie story demonstrates the reverence and power held by faeries for their names.

The story tells of an elf who twice helped an imprisoned maiden spin straw into gold for a greedy king. In fear for her life, she promised the elf her first-born child if he span the straw into gold for a third and final time. He agreed. The maid was saved from death and married the king, but reneged on her deal with the elf when her beautiful baby prince was born. The elf was livid but promised to free the queen from their contract if she guessed his name within three days.

After failing to work it out for two days running, desperate and afraid for her life, she crept into the forest on the second night in search of the elf's secret cottage. Eventually, she spied him dancing around a fire outside his cottage, gleefully singing:

> "Tonight, tonight, my plans I make,
> Tomorrow, tomorrow, the baby I take.
> The queen will never win the game,
> For Rumpelstiltskin is my name."

On the third day, the queen toyed with the elf, incorrectly guessing his name time after time. He hopped and danced with delight, but when she finally and triumphantly announced his actual name – "Rumpelstiltskin" – he flew into a fearsome rage.

The tale's finale varied in its level of gruesomeness, from Rumpelstiltskin flying out the window on a kitchen ladle to the retelling by the Brothers Grimm, in which he stamped his foot so hard in fury that one leg went through the splintered floor and he was torn in two! Regardless of the version, in the closing words, as those of many good faerie stories, "He was never to be seen again, and they all lived happily ever after."

SHHH! INDIRECT NAMES FOR FAERIES

Where faeries are nearby, it is said that you should never call them "faeries". Here are some well-known alternatives:

- **Wales**: The fair folk – *tylwyth teg*.
- **Ireland**: The little people, themselves, the good folk – *sídhe*.
- **Isle of Man**: The small people – *sleih beggey*.
- **Scotland**: Fair folk, wee folk, the good neighbours – *gude neighbours*.
- **Cornwall**: The small folk – *pobel vean*.
- **Iceland**: Hidden people – *huldufólk*.
- **Arabia**: The blessed ones – *mubarakin*.

✳ SPELLS AND COMMUNICATION ✳

There are records of ancient spells for summoning or seeing faeries. Many involve complex rituals and ingredients. In some rituals, speaking in Latin is recommended (although nobody can explain why faeries might speak Latin). Other spells or invocations come with a warning that the reality of seeing faeries is not what you might expect and could have you trembling with overwhelm.

A SPELL TO INVOKE A FAERIE

Here is a simplified summary of a spell written around the beginning of the seventeenth century, courtesy of *Percy's Reliques of Ancient English Poetry*, which is a collection of ballads, songs and poems. Percy pokes some gentle fun at the original author of the spell, which requires that first you know the name of a faerie (nearly impossible!), have some hen blood to hand, and that you are a pious person with good intentions.

1   Find a square crystal glass and pour the white of an egg into it.

2   Stand the glass in the blood of a white hen.

3   Leave it until three Wednesdays or three Fridays have passed.

4   Then, remove it and wash it in holy water to cleanse it.

5   Cut three hazel sticks of a year's growth.

6   Remove the bark and carve them so they are flat on one side.

7   Write the name of the faerie you wish to invoke on each stick.

8   Call the faerie's name three times.

9   Bury the glass and the sticks on a faerie hill.

10 Return to the same spot the following Wednesday
    or Friday (depending on which day you prepared
    them).

11 Dig up the glass and the sticks.

12 Be certain you are a clean-living person (pious and
    with good intentions).

13 Face to the east.

14 Call the faerie's name at 8 a.m. (or 3 p.m. or 10 p.m.,
    depending on the position of the planets in that
    quarter).

It is said that the faerie will reveal itself to you and be
bound to the glass to be called upon at other times.

FOUR-LEAFED CLOVERS AND THE GIFT OF FAERIE SIGHT

The four-leafed clover might be the most intriguing of all the plants with faerie powers. Confusingly, they are associated with:

- Protection from faeries.
- Enabling mortals to see faeries.
- Being a lucky charm.

As with so much in the world of the fae, nothing is as it seems. In one Victorian-era tale, a girl named Amelia was captured by dwarfs. She picked a four-leafed clover, which enabled her to escape back to the mortal world.

One tale in Robert Hun's 1865 book, *Popular Romances of the West of England*, a Cornish milkmaid put a pad of grass on her head to soften the weight of the milk pail she was carrying. A four-leafed clover was among the grass, which explained how she suddenly acquired the ability to see faeries. The family cow was a contented beast and had always given an exceptional yield. When the girl turned around, she noticed faeries swarming over it, patting and stroking the cow and happily helping themselves to drops of milk.

Horrified that her prize cow had a faerie infestation, the girl's mother painted the cow's udder with a vile concoction of salty brine and putrid fish stock. The faeries were never seen again, and the cow withered and died, pining for her faerie companions.

PRIMROSES: THE DOORWAY TO FAERIELAND OR DOOM?

In faerie lore, a posy of primroses on the threshold of your home will protect you from faerie mischief. In ancient woodlands, primrose patches are said to be the gateway to a flower faerie realm.

Brian Froud, author of the much-loved 1978 book *Faeries*, wrote that if you touch a faerie rock while holding the correct number of primroses, the entrance to Faerieland will open. But beware, for if you have the wrong number of primroses in your hand, a doorway to doom will open!*

*Clearly, it is best to avoid trying this spell as the right (or wrong) number is not stated, nor are there any details about identifying faerie rocks!

CHAPTER FOUR:
MEET THE FAERIES

Can you tell the difference between an elf and a pixie? Devoted folklorists have asked the same question, and, thanks to their hard work, a detailed classification of faeries now exists. Many types and subgenres of faeries, each with its own powers, locality and characteristics, have been carefully recorded.

If you think you know the faeries, think again! You'll discover beings with a penchant for stealing horses, and strange creatures who shed their furry outer skins and dance naked. One bad boy outranks the rest as the most wicked, and an endearing little fellow (who most of us assume is a faerie) belongs to an entirely different category. This chapter outlines some of the most well-known faeries, plus a few enchanting surprises.

✦ FAERIES (FAIRIES, FAE, FAY) ✦

ORIGIN
Ancient Greek, Persian, Slavic, Norse and Celtic mythology

APPEARANCE
Varies

HABITAT
A hinterland between the angelic and human realms

POWERS
Varies, but can include magic, shapeshifting, flight, telepathy, invisibility and immortality

CHARACTER AND TEMPERAMENT
Varies

GOOD OR BAD
Either, or a mixture of both

As we've established, faeries are generally considered mythical semi-humanoid beings with supernatural powers. Some even resemble animals and several can shapeshift. Many seem able to fly, live underwater, and pass through solid matter as if it were air. No wonder we are fascinated by them.

Faeries are even more intriguing because, on the whole, they are indifferent to the human race. Granted, a few will seek us out for company, and some enjoy causing us to suffer, but mostly they have their own thing going on!

Even their location is a mystery. If you think it possible that there are unseen parallel planes to the human one – an angelic realm, a spirit realm, a ghost realm – you might also consider the possibility of a magical faerie realm draped over the natural world.

Each type of faerie has its own characteristics, appearance and powers. Contrary to popular interpretation, few faeries have wands, and their environment shapes their physical nature – mountain dwarfs are sturdy and robust and flower faeries are delicate little things. As you can see, faerie species are anything but uniform.

✳ PIXIES (PISKIES, PIGSEYS) ✳

ORIGIN
South-west England and Ireland

APPEARANCE
Slender, less than two feet tall, with human features and ragged clothing

HABITAT
Grassy moorlands

POWERS
Can become invisible, communicate with animals, and create illusory effects on the landscape

CHARACTER AND TEMPERAMENT
Scampish, fun-loving and hardworking

GOOD OR BAD
Mostly good, though mischievous if offended

Pixies are earth faeries who live above ground. A wingless species of faerie, they are impish creatures with rather sharp, human facial features and slender bodies. They are no higher than two feet tall and perhaps as small as 12 inches. Their skin has a greenish hue, blending easily into natural surroundings. The Victorians depicted them as having pointed ears and eyes that slant upwards, but there is no earlier record of those features.

As folklore merged with Christianity, pixies in Devon and Cornwall were thought to be the souls of children who had died unbaptized. This is an entirely natural assumption, given that pixies are so childlike. They have a mischievous sense of playfulness, dancing, tumbling, and even wrestling with each other on the moors. Pixies have abundant energy and a carefree zest for fun. Magically benign, they have little need for potent magic other than the ability to become invisible, communicate with animals, and perhaps lead a clumsy traveller astray.

HARD WORK AND MISCHIEF

Aside from frolicking, pixies are hard workers and helpful to humans they consider worthy of assistance. There are tales of them helping with housework or threshing grain for friendly farmers in exchange for fresh bread and cheese. They are often ragged in appearance on account of their love of wrestling and playing on the moors.

Pixies have a natural affinity with horses. One of their favourite pastimes is stealing horses and riding them madly across the moors. A stolen – or "borrowed" – horse will return exhilarated from its gallop with its mane mysteriously tangled and knotted by tiny fingers.

Green and Lilliputian, a sleeping pixie can easily be mistaken for a tuft of grass. Anyone treading on one of those tufts will immediately lose all sense of direction. The pixie's magic will cause familiar landmarks to vanish into the ether, rendering the traveller disorientated and unable to find their way. This is where the phrase "pixie-led" is thought to have come from.

A CORNISH TALE

Before the mid-nineteenth century, the English county of Cornwall had numerous cultural depictions of pixies. One tale that demonstrates the hard work and mischief of pixies involves an aged Cornish widow who was the beneficiary of pixie kindness. They helped with chores, such as fetching water, sweeping and cleaning the hearth. In return, she fed them bread and honey, and it was a happy arrangement.

Yet the widow wanted to repay them further. She secretly hand-sewed exquisite little pixie suits. When the outfits were finished, she laid them out for the pixies to find in the morning. Instead of gratitude, they took umbrage, declaring that they were now too well-dressed to help a poor widow with her menial chores and left her to fend for herself.

"The Pixies know no sorrow, the Pixies feel no fear,
They take no care for harvest or seedtime of the year;
Age lays no finger on them, the reaper time goes by
The Pixies, they who change not, nor grow old or die."

Nora Chesson

✳ BROWNIES (HOUSE SPRITES) ✳

ORIGIN
Wales, Scotland, England and the Isle of Man

APPEARANCE
Wizened, weathered, about two feet tall with no nose and wearing a ragged tunic

HABITAT
Any home where they can offer useful service

POWERS
They can make themselves invisible

CHARACTER AND TEMPERAMENT
Humble, hardworking and helpful, but sensitive to criticism and will unleash violent mayhem if offended

GOOD OR BAD
Good and loyal, unless offended

Brownies are house sprites. Unkempt and unbothered by their appearance, brownies are not considered attractive in the faerie world. They have brown, wrinkled skin, straggly hair and thin arms. In place of a nose, there are just nostrils. They wear only raggedy clothes or tunics. They are solitary creatures, but they like the company of humans. Any person lucky enough to be adopted by a brownie will find them utterly loyal, domesticated and selfless.

While they have no attachment to possessions, they form strong attachments to whomever they choose to serve. They work tirelessly, provided that extreme care is taken not to offend them. A humble brownie can easily turn into a spiteful boggart once enraged.

As is the case with any house sprite, to pay a brownie for their labour is an insult. Instead, fresh cream and warm bread or honey cake can be left where the brownie might find them by chance. A parent feeding their child something delicious might sing:

"There's a piece wad please a brownie."
William Henderson, *Folk-Lore*
of the Northern Counties

THE TALE OF HAIRY MEG AND BROWNIE-CLOD

Most tales are of male brownies, except for the tale of the Scottish Highland brownie, Maggy Moulach – or Hairy Meg.

Maggy's only son, Brownie-Clod, was a dobie, a type of brownie not blessed with much intelligence. Together, they guarded the haunted and eerie Fincastle Mill in the Scottish Highlands. Late one stormy night, a girl was baking her wedding cake but was short of flour. Left with no option if she wanted to finish the cake, she braced herself and ventured out to Fincastle Mill.

Once inside, she lit the fire and put on a pot of water to boil while she ground the wheat. At midnight, Brownie-Clod appeared. He leered and asked her name. Disguising her fear and repulsion, she facetiously said her name was "Me Myself". He edged much closer to her, and she threw a ladle of boiling water over his foot to deter him.

Furious, he grabbed her, and she hurled the whole pot at him, boiling water and all. He screamed and fled to his mother. As he lay dying from the scalding, Maggy asked who had done that to him. He replied, "T'was Me Myself." Distraught that her son had scalded himself to death, Maggy was unable to find peace.

Some years later, the girl was boasting to friends of how she had killed the Brownie-Clod of Fincastle Mill. Maggy Moulach overheard every word. Furious, she avenged her son's death by throwing a wooden stool at the girl with such violence that it killed her in one blow.

Maggy fled to a faraway farm. She worked so diligently that the farmer dismissed all his farmhands, leaving the entire workload to Maggy. Offended and with a taste for revenge, she became a troublesome boggart with a mission. Maggy went on strike, and his farm began to fall to ruin. She watched on, delighted! Eventually though, he rehired the workers, and Maggy moved on.

✳ LEPRECHAUNS ✳

ORIGIN
Ireland

APPEARANCE
Less than two feet tall, red hair and beard, military coat, a three-cornered hat and silver buckles on their shoes

HABITAT
Rural areas, with their homes disguised as rabbit holes, or inside faerie trees

POWERS
Can turn faerie gold to leaves

CHARACTER AND TEMPERAMENT
Sly and wily, merry and mischievous

GOOD OR BAD
Not wholly good nor wholly evil

Leprechauns are solitary faeries famed for their cunning mischief and miserly ways. Native to the Emerald Isle, leprechauns are industrious in two ways: they hoard gold and make exquisite shoes. Faeries dance until their tiny shoes are worn away, so a skilled cobbler is never short of work. If you catch a leprechaun before he sees you, and you have your wits about you, he may lead you to a secret crock of gold... or play wicked tricks on you!

> "He's a span
> And a quarter in height.
> Get him in sight, hold him tight,
> And you're a made Man!"
> **William Allingham**

Modern leprechauns are depicted as harmless fellows in wide-brimmed tall hats. In folklore, they are wily characters who outwit more people than they help. Skinny and impish, they wear red or green military coats and three-cornered hats. When their shoe-cobbling work is done, they can turn from leprechauns into wild clurichauns who steal wine and drunkenly ride terrified sheep in the moonlight.

✶ BOGGARTS ✶

ORIGIN
Wales, Scotland, England and the Isle of Man

APPEARANCE
Less than two feet, hairy with long arms and a mean-looking, contorted face

HABITAT
Human homes, but sometimes under bridges or ditches

POWERS
Often invisible

CHARACTER AND TEMPERAMENT
Violent, aggressive and malevolent

GOOD OR BAD
Bad

Close relatives to brownies, boggarts are house spirits, though the similarity ends there. Compared to helpful brownies, boggarts are malevolent. It is a cursed and tragic household that is forced to tolerate them.

Some say that boggarts are brownies who have turned wicked after bad treatment. They become uncouth, violent and physically hideous. Lazy and spiteful, boggarts are often mistaken for poltergeists. Out of nowhere, objects fly through the air, children are pushed into cupboards, and bowls of porridge are upturned.

In one old Yorkshire folk tale, there lived a kind and gentle farmer called George Gilbertson. He and his family fled their farm to escape persecution by a violent boggart. They packed all their worldly goods onto their cart, only to find the boggart hiding in a milk churn tucked among their possessions. The boggart was going with them!

But fear not. If you have boggart trouble, be assured that they will eventually tire of their sport and move on.

✦ CHANGELINGS ✦

ORIGIN
Mainland Europe and Ireland

APPEARANCE
Sickly and like ugly, wizened babies

HABITAT
In mortal homes

POWERS
Takes on the appearance of a real baby

CHARACTER AND TEMPERAMENT
Fretful and feeble or demanding with a voracious appetite

GOOD OR BAD
The changeling is not always bad in itself, but the situation of finding one in your home is dire

A tale of a changeling baby is seldom happy. While many faeries wish no harm, it is not beyond them to commit heinous acts for the benefit of their own kind. The legend tells that fae would steal babies and replace them with a changeling because human babies add genetic fire and new blood to dwindling faerie communities. The changeling would be enchanted, so that to the parents, it would appear to be their own baby. But then the baby would curiously sicken or deform and perhaps even die. Other times, it was obviously a changeling and resembled a hideous old elf, or it was just a crude wooden carving of a baby.

Parents were left with horrible choices. At best, they could care kindly for the changeling, hoping their natural-born child would receive the same love in the faerie realm. Otherwise, the changeling would be thrown on the fire, whereupon it would fly up the chimney, cackling, and the true baby would be found alive on the doorstep.

✳ DWARFS ✳

ORIGIN
Germany, Switzerland and Scandinavia

APPEARANCE
Less than two feet tall, sturdy, bearded

HABITAT
Underground

POWERS
Invisibility, prophecy and imbuing objects with magical powers

CHARACTER AND TEMPERAMENT
Courageous, loyal, moral, gruff and hearty

GOOD OR BAD
Mostly good

Sturdy and industrious, dwarfs are associated with supernatural physical strength, powerful magic and craftsmanship. They live in subterranean halls and work in troops, usually mining for gold and jewels. When duty calls, they are also fierce warriors. Male dwarfs dominate the folklore, but occasionally, a dwarf wife, sister or child gets a small mention.

Dwarf craftsmanship is legendary, particularly their metalwork. Closely aligned with the world of wizards, magic and faeries, dwarfs make exquisite jewellery, crowns, swords and shields. Sometimes, the dwarfs will imbue an object with magical powers.

> "The dwarves of yore made mighty spells,
> While hammers fell like ringing bells
> In places deep, where dark things sleep,
> In hollow halls beneath the fells."
>
> **From the song "Far Over the Misty Mountains Cold", *The Hobbit*, J. R. R. Tolkien**

✴ ELVES ✴

ORIGIN
Iceland and the Faroe Islands

APPEARANCE
Tall, noble, elegant and beautiful

HABITAT
In a parallel dimension inside huge volcanic rocks

POWERS
Immortality (but can be slain by violence), telepathy and invisibility

CHARACTER AND TEMPERAMENT
Wise and intuitive

GOOD OR BAD
In ancient lore, mostly benevolent; in later lore, often mischievous and malevolent

Cute festive elves are an entirely modern phenomenon. Hollywood and storybooks tell of quirky little creatures in pointed hats. This is far removed from their origins. Elves in Norse and European mythology were tall, supernatural humanoid beings divided into light and dark elves... or good and evil elves. Beautiful and beguiling, humans were in awe of them. In Iceland, the words elf and *huldufólk* (hidden people) are still used interchangeably.

ICELANDIC ELVES

Imagine yourself in ancient Iceland, where life was bleak, poor and short. Children were often left for long periods in a dangerous landscape while their parents worked. Women were posted alone to remote locations to tend flocks.

In contrast to their brutally hard lives they believed in, a parallel, invisible world inhabited by a race of statuesque immortal elves wearing richly tapestried clothes and jewels. If a child went missing, then perhaps the elves had taken it. This comforted grieving parents because the elves would surely give the child a better life.

ROMANCING THE ELF

Also in Iceland, some women were said to be seduced by elves, even leading to pregnancies in some cases. It was said that the elves remained to help them give birth, and sometimes then spirited the newborn away to their hidden realm. Marriage between elves and mortals was forbidden, and both parties would forever mourn the loss of their lover.

All is not as it seems. These myths existed in a time when female infidelity and pregnancy out of wedlock were cruelly punished, abusive men often went unpunished, and child mortality was high.

LITTLE MISCHIEF MAKERS

Across the ocean, elves in the British Isles and Europe were believed to be capricious creatures best avoided, and more aligned with diminutive faeries. They would steal food and injure cattle or people with their weaponry (termed elf-shots), which were prehistoric flint tools or flint-tipped arrows. The sense of majesty and awe afforded their Icelandic cousins diminished along with the reduced physical size of European elves. There are many ancient tales of helpful or "light" elves, but elves were often considered dangerous.

Then, in Shakespeare's *A Midsummer Night's Dream*, the depiction of elves softens. Rather than the noble Icelandic elf, or his spiteful European counterpart, Puck is a prankster brimming with mischief, chaos and wit:

> **"I am that merry wanderer of the night.**
> **I jest to Oberon and make him smile."**

Some 350 years later, the elves created by J. R. R. Tolkien were entirely different from Shakespeare's interpretation and more characteristic of their ancient Icelandic forebears. Tolkien wrote of an immortal race, tall and exceptionally beautiful, beardless, wise and noble. With more than a wistful nod to the original mythology, he wrote, in *The Fellowship of the Ring*, that time moves both quickly and slowly for the elves: slowly, because they do not count the passing years, and quickly, as they do not change but the world around them continues to move forward. This, he wrote, "is a grief to them".

✳ GOBLINS ✳

ORIGIN
Anglo-Norman

APPEARANCE
Small, grotesque with a hideous grimace and yellow teeth

HABITAT
In grottos or caves, and occasionally in human homes

POWERS
Invisibility and physical strength beyond their size

CHARACTER AND TEMPERAMENT
Wicked, cunning and violent

GOOD OR BAD
Bad, bad, bad

Nothing about a goblin is pleasant. They are commonly malicious, grotesque little monsters. Bad to the bone, robbing faeries and mortal misery is their delight. Especially nasty are redcaps, who live in abandoned ruins on the Scottish borders. Passing travellers were brutally murdered, and their blood was used to dye the goblin's hat red. Redcaps must frequently kill people because they perish if the colour fades from their hats.

There's nothing like a villain to inspire storytellers. In 1859, Christina Rossetti wrote *Goblin Market* about two sisters and goblin fruit merchants. The poem is ripe with sexual overtones, forbidden fruit and Christian morality:

> "No," said Lizzie: "No, no, no;
> Their offers should not charm us,
> Their evil gifts would harm us."

More recently, goblins have evolved into less demonic characters and are associated with gold and mining. In Cornish folklore, some goblins were even helpful, and in the *Harry Potter* books wily goblins operate the high-security Gringotts Bank. However, the conventional wisdom remains that goblins should be avoided.

✴ GNOMES ✴

ORIGIN
Mainland Europe

APPEARANCE
Less than 12 inches, stocky, rotund and the males are bearded

HABITAT
Below Earth's surface in the Underland

POWERS
Guardians and carers of Earth's natural assets

CHARACTER AND TEMPERAMENT
Gentle and peaceful

GOOD OR BAD
Good

There is often confusion about dwarfs, goblins and gnomes. It is only polite to know the difference. You won't find gnomes in the fae realm because they belong to a different group called elementals. Gnomes exist in the Underland and can move through solid earth as if it were air. Their name is thought to derive from mid-seventeenth-century French from the Latin *gnomus*, which denotes a mythical race of very small people from Ethopia and India.

Gnomes are guardians of Earth's inherent natural treasures. For many humans, "treasure" means riches with a monetary value, and so gnomes came to be seen as guardians of gold and jewel mines. But rather than regarding them as treasure hoarders, we'd do better to place an ornamental gnome in a natural habitat, a far more accurate tribute to these peaceful, earthy elementals.

Elementals are spiritual representations of nature. The Swiss philosopher Paracelsus defined the elementals as follows:

"Gnomes tend the earth, sylphs control the flow of air, salamanders reside in fire and undines live in water."

✳ SEA AND WATER FAERIES ✳

ORIGIN
Europe, particularly Scandinavia

APPEARANCE
Often beautiful and enchanting

HABITAT
The Seven Seas, shorelines, rivers, lakes and pools

POWERS
Can bestow good fortune on kindly mortals, or whip up storms and wreck ships

CHARACTER AND TEMPERAMENT
Curious, playful or treacherous

GOOD OR BAD
Good if respected, otherwise vengeful

SELKIES

The gentlest of the sea faeries are the seal people or selkies, who originate from the folklore of the Orkney and Shetland Isles. In the Scottish Highlands they are called *roane*. In the water, they can easily be mistaken for seals, but even gentle selkies will avenge the slaughter of their kindred seals by whipping up storms.

The stories tell how fishermen would become entranced by elusive selkies who shed their outer seal bodies, or skins, revealing their inner human form as they sang and danced naked on the shore. If a human male were to steal a faerie's seal skin, he could capture her and make her his bride.

Selkies are sweet and helpful, and such marriages would last as long as the faerie's stolen seal skin remained hidden. But her innate yearning for the sea would overcome her if she found her seal skin. Then she would slip it on and return forever to the salty depths, leaving her mortal land-husband to pine.

MERPEOPLE

Merpeople are beautiful and beguiling, with silken hair, slender human bodies and sea-green eyes. In place of legs, they have a shimmering fish tail. Curious and capricious, female merpeople – mermaids – playfully seek the company of mortal men. At other times, innocent sailors would be entranced by the mermaids' beauty and by hypnotic music. The sailors would swim out to the mermaids, only to be dragged to the ocean floor, where the mermaids would savagely devour them. Conversely, mermen show no interest in humans other than avenging the death or capture of their kind by raising fierce storms and causing shipwrecks.

IRELAND'S MERROWS

Female merrows are as captivating as their mermaid cousins, but male merrows are grotesque, with green teeth and hair and pig-like facial features. They wear a magical red cap through which they have the power to breathe in air or water. Merrow males are jovial creatures, happy to entertain humans with tales of the sea – unless given cause to avenge the cruel treatment of fellow merrows, in which case they are ruthlessly merciless.

GWRAGEDD ANNWN

Gwragedd Annwn are female Welsh lake faeries, otherwise known as "wives of the lower world". They have a human form, elfin and beautiful, and are clothed in green dresses. It is thought that the Lady of the Lake (who returned the sword Excalibur to King Arthur) was *Gwragedd Annwn*. Mysterious and elusive, they are rarely seen, but legend tells of their benevolence towards worthy humans. These subaqueous fae may even take a mortal husband and live on land.

URISKS

Lonely and solitary, urisks are said to have lived on the edge of pools and waterfalls in the Scottish Highlands. They are small creatures, half goat, and with a hairy human-like upper body. Often desperate for company, they will tag along with anyone passing by. This seldom goes well. Humans usually flee, terrified by the urisk's goat legs, scraggy upper body and goat-like green face.

If their friendly approaches to humans are rejected, hurt and indignant, the urisk will disappear in a puff of magic smoke.

✳ SKRIKER ✳

ORIGIN
Yorkshire and Lancashire

APPEARANCE
Huge, hound-like with large feet

HABITAT
Woodland and forest

POWERS
Can cause death

CHARACTER AND TEMPERAMENT
Terrifying

GOOD OR BAD
Bad

There is debate as to whether skrikers are an unseelie faerie hound or a spectral ghost hound. Some say they are shapeshifting goblins who wander the forests at night, giving out fearful screams. The goblin becomes a ferocious hound with huge feet and glowing saucer eyes when it catches a mortal. Their poor victim will not survive.

Other times, skrikers are said to be the spirits of the dead who return in hound form to haunt specific humans for their mortal sins. One legend tells of a woman wrongly hanged as a witch in Hertfordshire, England. After her death, a black dog said to be a skriker haunted the gallows, howling into the night.

✴ SHELLYCOATS ✴

ORIGIN
Scotland

APPEARANCE
Huge creatures clothed in a coat covered with shells

HABITAT
Creeks, lakes and streams

POWERS
Benign

CHARACTER AND TEMPERAMENT
Mischievous

GOOD OR BAD
Harmless

According to Scottish folklore, shellycoats inhabit watery locations. They wear coats festooned with freshwater shells, which rattle and clatter as they move. Legend tells of two men once led by a voice calling, "Lost! Lost!" The friends searched all night along the riverbanks and trails following the voice. As day broke, they reached the source of the mournful cries. A shellycoat leapt down the opposite riverbanks, taunting and mocking them with his laughter and shaking his shell coat.

Another favourite shellycoat trick is to pretend they are drowning and then laugh loudly and applaud themselves when someone tries to save them. Shellycoats are harmless, apart from their perverse sense of fun.

✳ KNOCKERS ✳

ORIGIN
Cornwall

APPEARANCE
Short and stocky

HABITAT
Mines and caves

POWERS
Invisibility

CHARACTER AND TEMPERAMENT
Helpful but temperamental

GOOD OR BAD
Harmless

Knockers are subterranean, gnome-like creatures in Cornish and Devon folklore. They are believed to be generally friendly to miners and make a knocking sound where there is tin. According to legend, in one Cornish mine, knocking could be heard so deep in the mine that no man was prepared to go there. An old man and his son ventured out on Midsummer night and saw the small knockers bringing the ore up from the mine. The men agreed with the little miners that if they brought the tin up to the surface, the men would do the work of breaking up the ore. The men were to keep the richest stuff and leave one-tenth for the knockers.

The men were true to their word and the family became rich. But when the old man died, his son became greedy and stopped leaving what was due to the knockers. Cursed, the knockers ceased their work, and the son experienced a run of terrible bad luck. He soon took to drink and died penniless.

CHAPTER FIVE:
THE TWENTIETH CENTURY AND BEYOND

From the beginning of the twentieth century right up until the present day, faeries have remained culturally relevant. Parents help children pop their fallen teeth under the pillow for the Tooth Fairy, and Christmas elves in pointed hats are a cheery festive trope rolled out year after year.

Modern interpretations of faeries often have a benign quality, which is unsurprising given their makeover by the Victorians. Perhaps it was a form of escapism that saw painters and illustrators depict faeries as the ethereal gossamer-winged creatures familiar to us today. It appears that the nebulous and unpredictable faeries of yesteryear have been tamed... but, fortunately, not dulled. Faeries are having a renaissance!

CICELY MARY BARKER'S FLOWER FAIRIES

Cicely Mary Barker was the artist and illustrator responsible for the immensely successful series of books, *The Flower Fairies.*

Cicely was born in Croydon, England in 1895. At the age of 16, her father enrolled her into the Croydon Art Society, where she flourished as an artist. Her flower watercolour paintings are botanically accurate and exquisitely executed. Each flower has a corresponding tiny winged faerie, delicately dressed in harmony with it. Cicely's sister ran a nursery school from the back room of their house, and she used the children as models for the paintings. The faeries all have the innocence and rosy cheeks of pre-school children. The public was enchanted!

The Flower Fairies have endured for well over a hundred years with a global market in books and merchandise. Cicely's faeries are not from tales of lore, but there can be no doubt that her work did much to shape the modern perception of faeries.

✦ TINKER BELL ✦

In his 1904 play *Peter Pan*, J. M. Barrie opened up a glorious world for children. Tinker Bell and Peter flitted between Edwardian London and Neverland. Tinker Bell was an impetuous, capricious little character whose speech was made up of tinkling bells and could only be understood by people who spoke "fairy". Following Disney's release of the animated version of *Peter Pan*, Tinker Bell became a Disney icon, second only to Mickey Mouse.

✦ DISNEY'S DELIGHTFUL SINGING DWARFS ✦

Walt Disney Productions found a rich source of inspiration in faerie stories. *Snow White and the Seven Dwarfs* was released in 1937. It was the first feature-length animation and included songs, magic, romance and a good-overcoming-evil storyline.

Snow White is based on the Brothers Grimm faerie story, which they had adapted from ancient Germanic folklore. The original version was far more sinister and ugly, so much so that the Brothers Grimm toned it down.

J. R. R. TOLKIEN'S LEGENDARIUM

In contrast to Disney's family animations, J. R. R. Tolkien is acknowledged as the father of modern fantasy literature, or "high fantasy". A professor and fellow of Oxford University, a philologist, writer and poet, Tolkien produced an astounding volume of work.

Written in the 1930s, *The Hobbit* displayed Tolkien's vast understanding of mythology and legend. In the book, he took the dwarfs, wizards and dragons of lore and created an alternate realm called Middle Earth.

TOLKIEN FANDOM

As well as critical success, Tolkien's work has attained cult status. The Tolkien fandom is an international community of enthusiasts. Fans engage in discussions, create fan art, attend conventions, and engage in role-playing games inspired by Tolkien's work or "legendarium".

SIR ARTHUR CONAN DOYLE AND THE COTTINGLEY FAIRIES

Sir Arthur Conan Doyle (1859–1930) was the author of the famous Sherlock Holmes detective stories. Doyle had many interests, including spirituality, and he was a member of The Ghost Club, whose members shared an interest in the supernatural.

Conan Doyle's interests also extended to faeries. In 1917, two young girls named Elsie Wright and Frances Griffiths photographed faeries in their garden in Cottingley, England. Their photographs rapidly gained attention and, in a strange twist, Sir Arthur Conan Doyle became embroiled in the controversy surrounding them. He wrote about the Cottingley Fairies in an article for *The Strand Magazine*, expressing his belief that the photographs were authentic evidence of the existence of faeries. The public was divided, but fascinated!

COTTINGLEY FAKE NEWS

Decades later, however, it was proven that the photographs had been hoaxes. The girls had faked the photographs by cutting pictures of faeries from a children's book. They confessed that they hadn't set out to create a hoax, but the media interest, and then the support of a huge public figure like Sir Conan Doyle, had left the girls feeling that they had little choice but to go along with the story.

✴ **THE MODERN FAERIE** ✴

Even some pre-eminent thinkers about religion have opinions about faeries, and their opinions are a far cry from the damning views of King James VI.

IN THEOLOGY

The American theologian and philosopher David Bentley Hart has a fascinating take on whether or not to believe in faeries. He proposes that it is rational to accept that the world may consist of dimensions other than the singular dimension we see before us and that the other dimensions may even be more vital than our own.

He suggests that God, gods and faeries occupy the same space as cells, photons and the forces of gravity. To back up his case, Mr Hart argues that, once upon a time, there needed to be an expedition to prove the mere *existence* of tree frogs. Following that logic, science may well form an opinion on the existence of God, gods and faeries – once they get around to working out how to find them! Meanwhile, it would be arrogant in the extreme to suppose that there is nothing other than "us" on the planet.

SABINA MAGLIOCCO

Sabina Magliocco is an author and a professor of folklore, religion, neopaganism and witchcraft. In 2013, she suggested that today's faeries are more approachable and amicable than their ancestors.

In modern pagan and Wiccan folklore, faeries are depicted as spiritual aides, healers and guardians of nature. They give us glimpses into an enchanted world while cautioning us against environmental degradation.

FAERIE FESTIVALS

Renewed interest in paganism, white witchcraft and, yes, our friends the faeries, has led to an upsurge in literature, online groups and events. You don't have to search far to find a faerie festival.

The festivals celebrate all things fae with activities and attractions related to faerie folklore and fantasy. Visitors can immerse themselves in an escapist world of faerie-themed arts and crafts, storytelling sessions, live music and magical performances. Fantasy and costumes aside, these festivals provide an opportunity to connect with like-minded individuals who share an interest in faeries and folklore.

TWENTY-FIRST CENTURY CONTEMPORARY FAERIES

At the end of the twentieth century and into the twenty-first, contemporary witches and pagans have revived an interest in faeries. Rather than being locked into past traditions, they recognize that faeries play a different role in today's challenging world.

It's not just the pagans and witches who feel like this. Any gentle soul who holds spiritual beliefs and is concerned for the natural environment may sense that there is a secret Otherworld containing faeries who have changed and adapted to the modern environment.

At their core, these strange creatures are profoundly connected to nature. Many cultures identify them as guardians of the natural world. Recently, modern scientists discovered that some mushroom faerie rings are over 700 years old. Those curious fungal circles in the woods that we have been told not to enter or damage for fear of harming the faeries are more precious and more vulnerable than ever before. Humans like stories. They remind us to have a sense of wonder about the world around us.

✳ CONCLUSION ✳

Thank you for reading this book about peculiar creatures and curious events. This may be your first foray into the complex world of the fae. Some may say that faeries are mere whimsy, but there is no doubt that they are firmly entrenched in our past and in our present.

They are embedded in our past and traditions.

They are in our human backstory.

They are very much a part of us.

To believe in faeries is to connect with nature and the place between this world and another. Since antiquity, faeries have been regarded as intermediaries between humans and the divine. You don't have to look far to find significance in the symbolism and myths surrounding the faerie realm, or find other people utterly enchanted by the faeries.

You can now approach the wild, untamed world of the faeries with renewed interest. Open your senses and you'll feel their earthly yet unearthly presence. They'll thank you heartily for acknowledging them.

Close your eyes, breathe deeply and take a leap of faith. You won't be sorry.

"I do believe
in fairies!
I do! I do!"

J. M. BARRIE

✳ **FURTHER READING** ✳

Peter Pan in Kensington Gardens, J. M. Barrie,
illustrated by Arthur Rackham (Dover Children's
Classics, 2012)

The Complete Book of the Flower Fairies, Cicely Mary
Barker (Warne, 2002)

*An Encyclopedia of Fairies: Hobgoblins, Brownies,
Bogies, & Other Supernatural Creatures*, Katharine M.
Briggs (Allen Lane, 1976)

Faeries, Brian Froud and Alan Lee (Peacock Press,
Bantam Books, 1978)

Goblin Market, Christina Rossetti, illustrated by Arthur
Rackham (Pook Press, 2013)

Pre-Raphaelites: Tate Introductions
(Tate Publishing, 2012)

THE LITTLE BOOK OF FOLKLORE
Kitty Greenbrown

Paperback • ISBN: 978-1-83799-321-5

Folklore brings to life mythical creatures, fantastical knights and formidable spirits, and passes these stories down through the generations. From the famous Arthurian legends to monsters and fairies, explore the magical and mystical tales that have shaped the British Isles in this pocket guide. Filled with captivating stories of iconic characters like Robin Hood and Merlin, as well as lesser-known tales of giants and witches, this book will take you on a journey through this land of myth and legend.

THE LITTLE BOOK OF GODDESSES

Astrid Carvel

Paperback • ISBN: 978-1-80007-198-8

Embrace the power of the divine in this beginner's guide to some of mythology's fiercest females and most legendary ladies. Learn about Athena, the Greek goddess of wisdom and war; Bastet, the Egyptian goddess of pleasure and protection; Freyja, the Norse goddess of love, and many others. You'll be inspired and empowered by the tales of feminine power, strength and wisdom of all these dazzling deities.

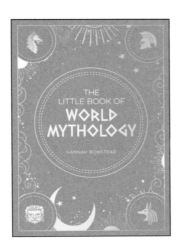

THE LITTLE BOOK OF WORLD MYTHOLOGY

Hannah Bowstead

Paperback • ISBN: 978-1-80007-176-6

Mythologies have been fundamental to cultures and societies throughout history and across the world. This pocket guide offers the perfect introduction to the major world mythologies, exploring their origins, foundational stories and key mythological figures. If you're looking to enrich and expand on your understanding of world history, religion and culture, then this book is an ideal starting point to fill your mind with stories of wisdom and wonder.

Have you enjoyed this book? If so, find us on Facebook at **Summersdale Publishers**, on Twitter/X at **@Summersdale** and on Instagram and TikTok at **@summersdalebooks** and get in touch. We'd love to hear from you!

www.summersdale.com

Image Credits

Star icons throughout © Kirill. Veretennikov/Shutterstock.com

pp.1, 3, 6, 28, 48, 74, 112, 122, 128 – cover images: leaves and butterfly wings © lyubava.21/Shutterstock.com

pp.9, 37, 53, 69, 71, 73 – mushrooms © Kirill.Veretennikov/Shutterstock.com

pp.13, 41, 42, 47, 68, 85, 111 – flowers, leaves and moons © Mirgunova/Shutterstock.com

pp.16, 21, 47, 56, 109, 118 – flowers and leaves © CholladaArt/Shutterstock.com

pp.17, 43, 51, 107 – mushrooms © Anastasia_ Panchenko/Shutterstock.com